I0695995

# LISTEN +
# LÜCKEN

Mik Berger

SONRRIE

**Einleitung – Leben in Listen**

ListenmacherInnen sind eine spezielle Spezies. Es beginnt ganz harmlos mit einer Einkaufsliste, entweder klassisch mit Stift und Zettel oder als Notiz auf dem Handy. Dann kommen die To-Do-Liste, die Geburtstageliste, die eine oder andere Pro-und-Contra-Liste. Die Gegenüberstellung von Einnahmen und Ausgaben lässt sich auch noch nachvollziehen. Typisch wird es, wenn überall im Haus die kleinen gelben Post-its hängen. Oder wenn sich neben der Liste der verflossenen LiebhaberInnen (natürlich mit Bewertungen) eine mit den Zahlen von 1 – 10 in dreißig verschiedenen Sprachen findet.

Vordergründig geht es um Organisation. Zeitmanagement, Tagesplanung, Kostenkontrolle. Dahinter steckt etwas anderes: Die Beruhigung der inneren Unruhe durch äußere Ordnung. Mit jedem Punkt, den man auf einer Liste durchstreicht, kommt man dem Ziel ein Stückchen näher. Um dann gleich eine neue Liste zu erstellen. Und weil alles zur Sucht werden kann, benennen wir das Ganze hiermit offiziell als Listensucht und dieses Buch als Suchtmittel.

**Oder ganz einfach: Listen sind Spaß. Jeder hat sich schon mal mit anderen über Fernsehserien aus der Kindheit, über beste Bücher, die Musik von früher oder Lieblingsessen unterhalten. Das alles und vieles mehr findet sich in mehr als 50 Listen in diesem Buch.** Gegenüber oder im Anschluss meist eine Liste zum Selbereintragen, allein oder zusammen mit anderen. Natürlich sind alle Listen höchst subjektiv, in der Reihenfolge nicht verbindlich und erheben keinen Anspruch auf Vollständigkeit. Wer es besser weiß oder ergänzen möchte – gerne. Viel Vergnügen!

**Los geht's mit den Listen!** 

## Essen von früher

1.      Kalter Hund

2.      Tote Oma/Grützwurst

3.      Hermann-Kuchen

4.      Arme Ritter

5.      Himmel und Erde

6.      Birnen, Bohnen und Speck

7.      Schmorgurken

8.      Falscher Hase

9.      Sternchensuppe

10.     Eier in Senfsoße

11.     Toast Hawaii

12.     Ragout Fin

13.     Soljanka

14.     Königsberger Klopse

15.     Kohlroulade

# Essen von früher – meine Liste:

1. _______________________________________________

2. _______________________________________________

3. _______________________________________________

4. _______________________________________________

5. _______________________________________________

6. _______________________________________________

7. _______________________________________________

8. _______________________________________________

9. _______________________________________________

10. _______________________________________________

11. _______________________________________________

12. _______________________________________________

13. _______________________________________________

14. _______________________________________________

15. _______________________________________________

# Süßes von früher

1.      Bärentatzen
2.      Schleckmuscheln
3.      Oblaten
4.      Treets
5.      Ahoi Brause-Pulver
6.      Goldmünzen
7.      PEZ
8.      Nappo
9.      Salinos
10.     Erfrischungsstäbchen
11.     Kaugummi aus dem Automaten
12.     Kuhbonbons
13.     Bazooka Bubble Gum
14.     Schokoladen-Zigaretten
15.     Prickel Pit
16.     Katzenzungen
17.     Luftschokolade
18.     Mäusespeck
19.     Zuckerwatte
20.     Capri-Eis

## Süßes von früher – meine Liste:

1. _______________________________________

2. _______________________________________

3. _______________________________________

4. _______________________________________

5. _______________________________________

6. _______________________________________

7. _______________________________________

8. _______________________________________

9. _______________________________________

10. _______________________________________

11. _______________________________________

12. _______________________________________

13. _______________________________________

14. _______________________________________

15. _______________________________________

## Wo wir eingekauft haben

1.    Beim Bäcker (beim Namen genannt)

2.    Beim Milchmann (Kanne - Glasflasche - Schlauch - Tetra Pak)

3.    Beim Fleischer/Schlachter („Eine Wiener für das Kind?")

4.    Am Kiosk (hatte auch einen Namen)

5.    Bei Spar (der auch!)

6.    Bei Aldi (was ganz Neues und so billig!)

7.    Bei Johs. Schmidt (Dr. Hillers Lakritz-Pfefferminz …)

8.    Bei Woolworth oder in der Kaufhalle („Nietenhosen")

9.    Bei Arko („Das ist nur ein bisschen angelaufen")

10.   Bei Schuh Kay (Elefanten oder Salamander Schuhe)

## Wo wir eingekauft haben:

1. _______________________________

2. _______________________________

3. _______________________________

4. _______________________________

5. _______________________________

6. _______________________________

7. _______________________________

8. _______________________________

9. _______________________________

10. _______________________________

## Das haben wir damals gespielt

Es gibt sie noch – die ganz einfachen Klassiker, die früher so einfach so viel Spaß gemacht haben. Aber mit Seltenheitswert. Hier sind sie:

1.    Gummitwist (meist auf dem Schulhof)

2.    Spitz pass auf!

3.    Elfer raus!

4.    Fang den Hut!

5.    Mau Mau

6.    Pochen

7.    Flohhüpfen

8.    Monopoly (klassisch)

9.    Scrabble

10.    Klabberjass (Norden)/Schafkopf (Süden)

11.    Mensch ärgere Dich nicht

10.    Memory (Kinder sind unschlagbar)

# Unsere Spieleklassiker:

1. _______________________________

2. _______________________________

3. _______________________________

4. _______________________________

5. _______________________________

6. _______________________________

7. _______________________________

8. _______________________________

9. _______________________________

10. _______________________________

## TV-Serien von damals

1. Immer wenn er Pillen nahm – Stanley Beamish, B-EE-I-L-E-N!

2. Mini-Max – Maxwell Smart alias Agent 86. Mel Brooks hatte seine Finger im Spiel.

3. Time Tunnel – die erste großartige SF-Serie.

4. Percy Stuart – „Ich werde mein Bestes tun", sagte Claus Wilcke.

5. Die seltsamen Methoden des Franz Josef Wanninger – Beppo Brem als Kriminalinspektor.

6. Graf Yoster gibt sich die Ehre – Lukas Amman als Graf und Wolfgang Völz als sein Diener.

7. Der Bastian – Paraderolle von Horst Janson und einem 2CV.

8. Arpad, der Zigeuner – deutsch-ungarisch-französische Co-Produktion

9. Salto Mortale – Zirkus-Serie mit Gustav Knuth, Hans Söhnker, Hellmut Lange, Hans-Jürgen Bäumler, Horst Janson u. v. a.

10. Der Geist und Mrs. Muir – sehr schöne Ghost Story

11.  Gilligans Insel – sieben Schiffbrüchige und das
     Chao

12.  Drei Mädchen und drei Jungen – Patchwork-
     Familie Brady und die einmalige Haushälterin
     Alice

13.  Mein Onkel vom Mars – Wann kommen end-
     lich die Wiederholungen?

14.  Mork vom Ork – Robin Williams als Außerir-
     discher

15.  Die Partridge Family – Teenie-Star David Cas-
     sidy im Tour-Bus

16.  Der Seewolf – mit Kartoffelquetscher Raimund
     Harmstorf

17.  Raumpatrouille – Die phantastischen Aben-
     teuer des Raumschiffes Orion

18.  UFO – S.H.A.D.O. kämpft gegen Außerirdi-
     sche

19.  Torchwood – Ähnliches Thema wie „UFO",
     außergewöhnlich umgesetzt

20.  Ein Colt für alle Fälle – Lee Major als Stunt-
     man und Kautionsjäger

# TV-Tier-Serien von damals

1. Daktari (1966 - 69) – mit Schimpansin Judy und Clarence, dem schielenden Löwen

2. Flipper (1964 - 67) – Sandy und Bud, die Söhne von Porter Ricks, rufen ihren Delfin mit der Unterwasserhupe.

3. Lassie (1954 - 73) – Eine Collie-Hündin als Retterin in der Not.

4. Fury (1955 - 60) – ein Waisenjunge und ein wilder Mustang

5. Rin Tin Tin (20er-Jahgre) – ein deutscher Schäferhund

6. Skippy, das Buschkänguruh (1966 - 68) – natürlich eine australische Serie

7. Boomer, der Streuner (1980 - 82) – Ein zotteliger Mischlingshund streunt durch die USA.

8. Mr. Ed (1961 - 66) – das sprechende Comedy-Pferd

9. Ein Platz für Tiere (D 1956 - 87) – 175 x Wissen, vermittelt von Prof. Bernhard Grzimek.

10. Im Reich der wilden Tiere (1963 - 88) – Dokumentationen

## Noch mehr Fernsehserien:

1. _______________________________

2. _______________________________

3. _______________________________

4. _______________________________

5. _______________________________

6. _______________________________

7. _______________________________

8. _______________________________

9. _______________________________

10. _______________________________

11. _______________________________

12. _______________________________

13. _______________________________

14. _______________________________

15. _______________________________

## Beste Western – Serien und Filme

1. Spiel mir das Lied vom Tod (1968)

2. 12 Uhr Mittags /High Noon (1952)

3. Zwei Banditen – Butch Cassidy und the Sundance Kid (1969)

4. Die glorreichen Sieben (1960/2016)

5. Rio Bravo (1959)

6. Für eine Handvoll Dollar (1964)

7. Bonanza (1959 - 73)

8. Big Valley (1965 - 69)

9. High Chaparral (1967 - 71)

10. Mein Name ist Nobody (1973)

11. Die Maske des Zorro (1998)

12. Django (1966)

13. Vier Fäuste für ein Halleluja (1971)

14. Der mit dem Wolf tanzt (1990)

15. Westworld (1973)

16. Bandidas (2006)

17.     Wild Wild West (1999)

18.     Cowboys & Aliens (2011)

19.     The Revenant - Der Rückkehrer (2015)

20.     _______________________________________

21.     _______________________________________

22.     _______________________________________

23.     _______________________________________

24.     _______________________________________

# TV-Serien für Kinder

1. Kli-Kla-Klawitter

2. Robbi, Tobbi und das Fliewatüüt

3. Plumpaquatsch

4. Barbapapa

5. Sesamstraße

6. Pan Tau

7. Lolek und Bolek

8. Die rote Zora und ihre Bande

9. Pippi Langstrumpf

10. Timm Thaler

11. _______________________

12. _______________________

13. _______________________

14. _______________________

15. _______________________

# Zeichentrickserien für Kinder

1. Die Biene Maja
2. Heidi
3. Wickie und die starken Männer
4. Pinocchio
5. Sindbad
6. Tom und Jerry
7. Bugs Bunny – Mein Name ist Hase
8. Der Rosarote Panther
9. Die Peanuts
10. Alice im Wunderland
11. Mila Superstar
12. Als die Tiere den Wald verließen
13. Die Gummibärenbande
14. Der kleine Maulwurf
15. Saber Rider und die Star Sheriffs

16. _______________________________

17. _______________________________

18. _______________________________

19. _______________________________

20. _______________________________

## Lieblingsfilme

1. Hausboot (1958), mit Sophia Loren und Cary Grant

2. Alexis Zorbas (1964), mit Anthony Quinn und Irene Papas, Musik Mikis Theodorakis

3. Tatsächlich Liebe (2003), mit Hugh Grant, Liam Neeson, Colin Firth, Emma Thompson …

4. Star Wars (ab 1977), mit Harrison Ford, Mark Hamill, Carrie Fisher u. a.

5. Der Herr der Ringe (2001 - 2003), mit Elijah Wood, Viggo Mortensen, Orlando Bloom u. a.

6. Pulp Fiction (1994), von und mit Quentin Tarrantino, mit John Travolta, Uma Thurman, Samuel L. Jackson, Bruce Willis, Harvey Keitel

7. Schindlers Liste (1993) von Steven Spielberg, mit Liam Neeson, Ralph Fiennes, Ben Kingsley

8. Einer flog über das Kuckucksnest (1995), mit Jacks Nicholson, Danny DeVito u. a.

9. Forrest Gump (1994), von Robert Zemeckis, mit Tom Hanks in der Hauptrolle

10. Die Goonies (1985), von Richard Donner

# Unsere Lieblingsfilme:

1. _________________________________

2. _________________________________

3. _________________________________

4. _________________________________

5. _________________________________

6. _________________________________

7. _________________________________

8. _________________________________

9. _________________________________

10. _________________________________

## Unvergessliche Filmzitate

1.  „Schau mir in die Augen, Kleines!" sagt Rick (Humphrey Bogart) zu Ilsa (Ingrid Bergman), wenn er ihr in *Casablanca* (1942) zuprostet. Bringt ja sonst auch Unglück. Ebenso wie in der neueren Fassung „Ich seh' dir in die Augen, Kleines!" eine freie Übersetzung.

2.  „Liebe bedeutet nie um Verzeihung bitten zu müssen". Große Gefühle in *Love Story* (1970), gespielt von Ali McGraw und Ryan O'Neal.

3.  „Sagen Sie nichts gegen Masturbation. Es ist Sex mit jemandem, den man wirklich mag." Alvy Singer (Woody Allen) in *Der Stadtneurotiker* (1977).

4.  „Ich bin dein Vater" – Darth Vader zu Luke Skywalker (Mark Hamill) in *Star Wars – Das Imperium schlägt zurück* (1980). „Möge die Macht mit dir sein!"

5.  „Nach Hause telefonieren" will *E.T. – Der Außerirdische* im gleichnamigen Film (1982), der frühe Beginn der Filmkarriere von Drew Barrymore als Gertie.

6.  „Hasta la vista baby": Arnold Schwarzenegger als Terminator in *Terminator 2 – Tag der Ab-*

*rechnung* (1991). „Ich komme wieder" müsste
aus dem ersten *Terminator* (1984) sein, kam
aber später wieder …

7.  „Es kann nur einen geben." Und das ist Connor MacLeod (Christopher Lambert) in *Highlander* (1986).

8.  „Mein Name ist Inigo Montoya. Du hast meinen Vater getötet. Jetzt bist du des Todes." Aus *Die Braut des Prinzen* (1987) nach dem Buch „Die Brautprinzessin". Da kann man schon mal Ärger bekommen, wenn man das als Fluggast auf dem T-Shirt stehen hat …

9.  „Ich habe eine Wassermelone getragen." Die geistreiche Antwort von „Baby" (Jennifer Grey) in *Dirty Dancing* (1987).

10. „Ich will genau das, was sie hatte!" Die Tischnachbarin, nachdem Sally (Meg Ryan) Harry (Billy Crystal) in *Harry & Sally*(1989) im Fastfood-Restaurant einen Orgasmus vorgespielt hat.

11. „Das Leben ist wie eine Schachtel Pralinen. Man weiß nie, was man kriegt." zitiert Forrest Gump (Tom Hanks) in *Forrest Gump* (1994) seine Mutter.

12.     „Houston, wir haben ein Problem“ ist eigentlich kein Filmzitat aus *Apollo 13* (1995)Tom Hanks als Jim Lovell), sondern ein Zitat aus Apollo 13.

13.     „Ich bin der König der Welt!“ Das ist natürlich Jack Dawson (Leonardo diCaprio) in *Titanic* (1997). Allerdings zeitlich eng begrenzt.

14.     „Ich bin doch nur ein Mädchen, das vor einem Jungen steht und ihn bittet, es zu lieben.“ So schön … Schauspielerin Anna Scott (Julia Roberts) und William Thacker (Hugh Grant) finden sich in *Notting Hill* (1999).

15.     „Willst du in mein Höschen? Da ist schon ein Arschloch drin!“ War das Goldie Hawn? Oder Meg Ryan? In welchem Film?

16.     _______________________________________

17.     _______________________________________

18.     _______________________________________

19.     _______________________________________

20.     _______________________________________

# Filmszenen für die Ewigkeit

1. Der Auftritt von Barry White in **Ally McBeal**. Die Grundidee super, der gemeinsame Tanz in der Unisex-Toilette großartig und der persönliche Auftritt in der Bar die Krönung.

2. Die gesamte Szene im portugiesischen Restaurant in **Tatsächlich Liebe**. Besonders schön: Die Übersetzungen.

3. Das Duell zwischen Zorro (Antonio Banderas) und Elena Montero (Catherine Zeta-Jones) in **Die Maske des Zorro**.

4. Die berühmte Szene in **Harry und Sally** im Fast-Food-Restaurant und die Dame vom Nebentisch: „Ich will genau das, was sie hatte!"

5. Marilyn Monroe über dem U-Bahn-Schacht in **Das verflixte 7. Jahr**.

6. Die Hier-ist-Johnny-Szene mit Jack Nicholson in **Shining** – als er nach den Axt-Schlägen durch die Tür guckt.

7. Neben den großartigen Dialogen mit Mrs. Robinson (Anne Bancroft) und dem spektakulären Soundtrack von Simon & Garfunkel in **Die Reifeprüfung** die Szene, als Benjamin (der

junge Dustin Hoffman) am Kirchenfenster steht. Und anschließend im Bus.

8.  Gene Kelly singing in the rain „Singin' in the Rain" in **Singin' in the Rain**.

9.  Oft kopiert: Die Anfangsszene von **Der weiße Hai** mit der ganz speziellen Musik.

10. **Blues Brothers** – insgesamt ganz groß. Witzige Szene neben dem endlosen Massen-Crash: Als er sie wieder in den Matsch fallen lässt.

11. Der Priester in **Harold and Maude** von 1971: „Dem welken Fleisch, den schlaffen Brüsten und schlappen Gesäßbacken …"

13. Der Tanz von Selma Hayek in der Titty Twister Bar in **From Dusk Till Dawn**.

14. **Spiel mit das Lied vom Tod**: auf der Mundharmonika und mit seinem Vater auf den Schultern.

15. Der Tanz in **Dirty Dancing** von Baby (Jennifer Grey) und Johnny (Patrick Swayze).

## Szenen, die ich immer wieder sehen könnte:

1. _______________________________

2. _______________________________

3. _______________________________

4. _______________________________

5. _______________________________

6. _______________________________

7. _______________________________

8. _______________________________

9. _______________________________

10. _______________________________

# TV-Shows von damals

1. Wünsch Dir was – Vivi Bach und Dietmar Schönherr

2. Einer wird gewinnen – Hans-Joachim Kulenkampff

3. Die Montagsmaler – Frank Elstner, Sigi Harreis u. a.

4. Am laufenden Band – Rudi Carrell

5. Zum Blauen Bock – Heinz Schenk

6. Dalli Dalli – Hans Rosenthal

7. Musik ist Trumpf – Peter Frankenfeld

8. Der goldene Schuss – Lou van Burg, Vico Torriani

9. Der große Preis – Wim Thoelke

10. Zwischenmahlzeit – Gisela Schlüter

11. __________________________________

12. __________________________________

13. __________________________________

## Game-Show-Klassiker

1. Glücksrad – Peter Bond, Frederic Meisner und Maren Gilzer (u. a.)

2. Der Preis ist heiß – Harry Wijnvoord und Walter Freiwald

3. Riskant/Jeopardy – Hans-Jürgen Bäumler/Frank Elstner

4. Bingo – Wolf-Dieter Herrmann

5. Geh auf's Ganze – Jörg Draeger und der Zonk

6. Ruck Zuck – Werner Schulze-Erdel/Jochen Bendel/Oliver Geissen u. a.

7. Familienduell – Werner Schulze-Erdel

8. Stadt, Land, Fluß – Victor Worms

9. Jeder gegen Jeden – Hans-Hermann Gockel/Holger Speckhahn

10. Wer wird Millionär? – Günther Jauch

11. Herzblatt – Rudi Carell/Reinhard Fendrich

12. Spiel ohne Grenzen – Camillo Felgen/Michael Schanze u. a

13.    Donnerlippchen – Jürgen von der Lippe

14.    Was bin ich? – Robert Lembke und „Welches
       Schweinderl hätten Sie denn gern?"

15.    Geld oder Liebe – Jürgen von der Lippe

16.    _______________________________________

17.    _______________________________________

18.    _______________________________________

19.    _______________________________________

20.    _______________________________________

# Die schrägsten Filmklassiker, Rollen und Schauspieler

1.  "Hellzapoppin - In der Hölle ist der Teufel los", US-Musical-Kommödie von 1941

2.  Die Filme der Marx-Brothers (1929 - 57), besonders Groucho Marx

3.  Die Filme mit Claudette Colbert, 30er-/40er-Jahre

4.  "Arsen und Spitzenhäubchen" (1944) mit Cary Grant, die zwei Tanten!

5.  "Leoparden küsst man nicht" (1938) mit Katharine Hepburn und Cary Grant

6.  "Unternehmen Petticoat" (1959) mit Tony Curtis und Cary Grant

7.  "Mein Freund Harvey" (1950) mit James Stewart

8.  Die Agatha-Christie-Filme mit Miss Marple (Margaret Rutherford, 30er-/40er-Jahre)

9.  "Manche mögen's heiß" (1959) von Billy Wilder, mit Marilyn Monroe und Tony Curtis

10.    "Bezaubernde Jeannie" (1960er-/70er-Jahre)
       mit Barbara Eden und Larry Hagman

## Noch mehr schräge Filme/Serien, Rollen und Darsteller

1.    "Kentucky Fried Movie", die erste und beste
      von mehreren John-Landis-Komödien

2.    "Das Leben des Brian" (GB 1979) mit John
      Cleese und Graham Chapman, Titelsong:
      "Always Look On The Bright Side Of Life"

3.    "Boston Legal", US-Anwaltsserie mit dem
      Dreamteam Denny Crane (William Shatner),
      Alan Shore (James Spader) und Shirley
      Schmidt (Candice Bergen)

4.    "Ally McBeal", die herrlich schräge US-
      Anwaltsserie, die Calista Flockhart zum Star
      machte. Mit Gastauftritten u. a. von Barry
      White, Gloria Gaynor, Anastacia, Tom Ber-
      enger, Jon Bon Jovi, Mariah Carey, Elton John,
      Sting, Dame Edna, Bruce Willis, Chubby
      Checker …

5.    Serenity/Firefly. Sci-Fi mal anders. Professio-
      nelle Weltraum-Plünderer im Jahr 2507, Uni-
      versalsprachen Englisch und Chinesisch.

6.      "Shaun das Schaf" (GB seit 2007). Ausnahme-
        leistungen auf dem Stop-Motion-Gebiet. Die
        eigentliche Hauptrolle hat Hund Bitzer.

7.      "Guardians of the Galaxy" (seit 2014). Setzt
        neue Maßstäbe im humorvollen SF-Genre.

8.      "Hotel Transsilvanien" (seit 2012), großartige
        Animations-Filmserie, im Original mit den
        Stimmen von Adam Sandler, Selena Gomez u.
        a. Als Synchronsprecher sind z. B. Rick Kava-
        nian und Elyas M'Barek dabei.

9.      "Lissi und der wilde Kaiser" (D 2007), ein
        Meisterwerk von Michael "Bully" Herbig

10.     "Ein Fisch namens Wanda" (1988) mit John
        Kleese, Kevin Kline und Jamie Lee Curtis

11.     _______________________________________

12.     _______________________________________

13.     _______________________________________

14.     _______________________________________

15.     _______________________________________

# Die besten Serien von Netflix, Prime, Disney+ & Co.

1.      Haus des Geldes

2.      Lilyhammer

3.      Orange Is The New Black

4.      The Night Manager

5.      You – Du wirst mich lieben

6.      Narcos

7.      Marvel's Agents of S.H.I.E.L.D.

8.      Lupin

9.      Game of Thrones

10.     Der Malorianer

11.     Lost In Space – Verschollen zwischen fremden Welten

12.     Game of Thrones

13.     Boston Legal

14.     Smalville

15.     firefly

# Die besten (oder neuere) Serien für mich:

1. _______________________________

2. _______________________________

3. _______________________________

4. _______________________________

5. _______________________________

6. _______________________________

7. _______________________________

8. _______________________________

9. _______________________________

10. _______________________________

11. _______________________________

12. _______________________________

13. _______________________________

14. _______________________________

15. _______________________________

## Unvergessene Werbesprüche

1.      Läuft und läuft und läuft … (VW)

2.      Nur nicht gleich in die Luft gehen (HB)

3.      Schönes Haar ist dir gegeben, lass es leben mit Gard

4.      Damit Sie auch morgen noch kraftvoll zubeißen können (blend-a-med)

5.      Ich will so bleiben wie ich bin (Du darfst)

6.      Mein Hüfthalter bringt mich um (Playtex)

7.      An meine Haut lasse ich nur Wasser und CD

8.      Sie baden gerade Ihre Hände darin (Palmolive)

9.      Drei Dinge braucht der Mann: Feuer, Pfeife, Stanwell

10.    Wer hat's erfunden? (Ricola)

11.    Dann klappt's auch mit dem Nachbarn (Calgonit)

12.    Schmilzt in der Hand und nicht im Mund (Treets)

13.    Bezahlen Sie einfach mit Ihrem guten Namen
       (American Express)

14.    Das verrückte Huhn ruft wieder an (Mc Do-
       nalds)

15.    So wertvoll wie ein kleines Steak (Fruchtzwer-
       ge)

16.    Ich habe gar kein Auto (Nescafé)

17.    Innen gut, außen mit Hut. (Sierra Tequila)

18.    Visa – die Freiheit nehm ich mir

19.    Komm doch mit auf den Underberg

20.    Für das Beste am Mann (Gillette)

## Ich erinnere mich auch an diese Werbung:

1.    ______________________________________________

2.    ______________________________________________

3.    ______________________________________________

4.    ______________________________________________

5.    ______________________________________________

6.    ______________________________________________

## Figuren aus der Werbung:

1. Das HB-Männchen

2. Die Lila Kuh von Milka

3. Meister Proper

4. Der Michelin-Mann

5. Der Duracell-Hase

6. Klementine (Ariel)

7. Der Wüstenrot-Fuchs

8. Der Bärenmarke-Bär

9. Lurchi (Salamander)

10. Der Trigema-Affe

11. Der Weiße Riese

12. Der Charmin-Bär

13. Tilly (Palmolive)

14. Der Marlboro-Mann

15. Der Melitta-Mann

## Da gibt es noch viele – zum Beispiel:

1. _______________________________________

2. _______________________________________

3. _______________________________________

4. _______________________________________

5. _______________________________________

6. _______________________________________

7. _______________________________________

8. _______________________________________

9. _______________________________________

10. _______________________________________

11. _______________________________________

12. _______________________________________

13. _______________________________________

14. _______________________________________

15. _______________________________________

**Bücher, die man gelesen haben muss**

1.      William Goldman: Die Brautprinzessin

2.      Carlos Ruiz Zafón: Der Schatten des Windes

3.      John Irving: Das Hotel New Hampshire

4.      Boris Vian: Der Schaum der Tage

5.      Douglas Adams: Per Anhalter durch die Galaxis

6.      Daniel Defoe: Robinson Crusoe

7.      Antoine de Saint-Exupéry: Der kleine Prinz

8.      James Redfield: Die Prophezeiungen von Celestine

9.      Karl May: Winnetou 1-3

10.     Anne Frank: Das Tagebuch der Anne Frank

11.     Jostein Gaarder: Sofies Welt

12.     Emmy von Rhoden: Der Trotzkopf

13.     James F. Cooper: Der letzte Mohikaner

14.     Henri Charrière: Papillon

15.     Mark Twain: Die Abenteuer des Tom Sawyer

# Das sind meine Lieblingsbücher:

1. ___________________________________________

2. ___________________________________________

3. ___________________________________________

4. ___________________________________________

5. ___________________________________________

6. ___________________________________________

7. ___________________________________________

8. ___________________________________________

9. ___________________________________________

10. ___________________________________________

11. ___________________________________________

12. ___________________________________________

13. ___________________________________________

14. ___________________________________________

15. ___________________________________________

## Populäre Comics, die man kennen muss

1.      Asterix der Gallier

2.      Micky Maus/Donald Duck etc.

3.      Tim & Struppi

4.      Prinz Eisenherz

5.      Superman

6.      Spirou & Fantasio

7.      Lucky Luke

8.      Die Peanuts

9.      Nick Knatterton

10.     Das Marsupilami

11.     Das Phantom

12.     Batman & Robin

13.     Die Abenteuer von Jo, Jette und Jocko

14.     Michel Vaillant

15.     Bessy

# Es gibt noch viel mehr gute Comics:

1. _______________________________________

2. _______________________________________

3. _______________________________________

4. _______________________________________

5. _______________________________________

6. _______________________________________

7. _______________________________________

8. _______________________________________

9. _______________________________________

10. ______________________________________

11. ______________________________________

12. ______________________________________

13. ______________________________________

14. ______________________________________

15. ______________________________________

# Die Jahrzehnte

**Das sind die Jahrzehnte für mich:**

1.      1940er – _______________________________

2.      1950er – _______________________________

3.      1960er – _______________________________

4.      1970er – _______________________________

5.      1980er – _______________________________

6.      1990er – _______________________________

7.      2000er – _______________________________

8.      2010er – _______________________________

9.      2020er – _______________________________

10.     2030er – _______________________________

## Wörter des Jahres

**2021** Wellenbrecher

**2020** Corona-Pandemie

**2019** Respektrente

Ermittelt von der Gesellschaft für deutsche Sprache e. V. in Wiesbaden. Vorschläge über www.gfds.de

## Unwörter des Jahres

**2021** Pushback

**2020** Rückführungspatenschaften/Corona-Pandemie

**2019** Klimahysterie

Ermittelt von vier Sprachwissenschaftler:innen und einer Journalistin

## Jugendwörter des Jahres

**2021** Cringe

**2020** Lost

**2018** Ehrenmann/Ehrenfrau

Ermittelt vom Pons Verlag, Jury/Jugendliche über die Website

# Die besten Musiker aller Zeiten

1. The Beatles

2. The Rolling Stones

3. Carlos Santana

4. Eric Clapton

5. David Bowie

6. Elton John

7. Talking Heads

8. Bob Marley

9. Prince

10. Pink Floyd

11. ______________________

12. ______________________

13. ______________________

14. ______________________

15. ______________________

## Ganz besondere Songs

1. Janis Joplin: Me and Bobby McGee

2. Santana: Samba pa ti

3. John Lennon: Imagine

4. George Harrison: My Sweet Lord

5. T. Rex: Hot Love

6. Led Zeppelin: Stairway To Heaven

7. Pink Floyd: Shine On You Crazy Diamond

8. Deep Purple: Paranoid

9. David Bowie: Heroes

10. Cat Stevens: Father And Son

11. Orchestral Manoeuvres In The Dark (OMD): Enola Gay

12. Fleetwood Mac: Dreams

13. Chicago: Hard To Say I'm Sorry

14. Nazareth: Love Hurts

15. Bob Dylan: Knocking On A Heavens Door

16. The Beatles: Hey Jude

17.     Simon & Garfunkel: The Sound Of Silence

18:     Rob Grill: Rock Sugar

19.     Juan Bastos: Loop Di Love

20.     Adriana Celentano: Yuppi Du

**„Anders" besonders:** „Und deine Tränen waren Ka-
jal" von Bosse, „Are we human or are we dancer" von
The Killers, „Der Himmel ist blau, komm, das machen wir auch" von Amanda, „Knutschfleck" von Ixi
und „Heroes" auf Deutsch von David Bowie.

## Meine/Unsere besonderen Songs:

1.     __________________________________________

2.     __________________________________________

3.     __________________________________________

4.     __________________________________________

5.     __________________________________________

6.     __________________________________________

7.     __________________________________________

8.     __________________________________________

## Deutsche Schlager für die Ewigkeit

1. Drafi Deutscher: Marmor, Stein und Eisen bricht

2. Marianne Rosenberg: Er gehört zu mir

3. Udo Jürgens: Griechischer Wein

4. Roy Black: Ganz in Weiß

5. Wencke Myhre: Er hat ein knallrotes Gummiboot

6. Cliff Richard: Rote Lippen soll man küssen

7. Karel Gott: Die Biene Maja

8. Manuela: Schuld war nur der Bossa Nova

9. Juliane Werding: Wenn du denkst du denkst dann denkst du nur du denkst

10. Helene Fischer: Atemlos durch die Nacht

11. DJ Ötzi & Nik P.: Ein Stern (der deinen Namen trägt)

12. Dschingis Khan: Moskau

13. Matthias Reim: Verdammt ich lieb dich

14. Nina Hagen: Du hast den Farbfilm vergessen

# Meine/Unsere Schlager-Favoriten:

1. _______________________________________
2. _______________________________________
3. _______________________________________
4. _______________________________________
5. _______________________________________
6. _______________________________________
7. _______________________________________
8. _______________________________________
9. _______________________________________
10. _______________________________________
11. _______________________________________
12. _______________________________________
13. _______________________________________
14. _______________________________________

# Sehr spezielle deutschsprachige Musiktitel

1. Trio: Da Da Da ich lieb dich nicht …

2. Foyers des Arts: Eine Königin mit Rädern untendran

3. Interzone: Ich und mein Freund die Katze

4. Joachim Witt: Ich bin der deutsche Neger

5. Erste Allgemeine Verunsicherung: Küss' die Hand, schöne Frau

6. Humpe & Humpe: Yama-ha

7. Edo Zanki: Viertel vor Neun Viertel vor Zehn

8. Markus: Ich will Spaß

9. Ina Deter: Ob blond, ob braun, ob henna

10. Ixi: Der Knutschfleck

11. Geier Sturzflug: Bruttosozialprodukt

12. Ludwig Hirsch: Schick di doch selber deiner Freundin in an Packerl

13. Hannes Wader: Ankes Bioladen

14. Franz Josef Degenhard: Geh doch in die Oberstadt

15.     Rio Reiser: König von Deutschland

16.     Culcha Candela: Hamma

17.     Heinz Rudolf Kunze: Sicherheitsdienst

18.     Esther & Abi Ofarim: Noch einen Tanz

19.     Marius Müller-Westernhagen: Marion aus
        Pinneberg

20.     Die Toten Hosen: Eisgekühlter Bommerlunder

## Da fällt mir noch mehr zu ein:

1.     _______________________________________________

2.     _______________________________________________

3.     _______________________________________________

4.     _______________________________________________

5.     _______________________________________________

6.     _______________________________________________

7.     _______________________________________________

8.     _______________________________________________

9.     _______________________________________________

## Songs, die akustisch gern falsch verstanden werden

1. **Que será – nie wieder!** Que Será Mi Vida von den Gibson Brothers

2. **Wann kommt die Sahne?** Gib mir Sonne von Rosenstolz

3. **Mit knallharten Champagnerfäden** Geiles Leben von Glasperlenspiel

4. **Sie geht aus und ich schlaf ein** Counting Stars von One Republic („Seek it out and ye shall find")

5. **Ich ruf jeden an, denn ich Candy** Drei Uhr Nachts von Mark Foster + LEA

6. **Du musst besoffen bestellen** I Just Died In Your Arms Tonight von Cutting Crew („It must have been something you said")

7. **Niemand kann das bezahlen** Laura Non C'È („Mi manca da spezzare")

8. **Du blöde Sau** Bad von Michael Jackson („The world is out")

9. **Da geht der Gärtner** Dirty Diana von Michael Jackson

10. **Es tobt der Hamster vor meinem Fenster**

Pflaster von Ich + Ich („Es tobt der Hass da")

## Songs, die inhaltlich gern falsch verstanden werden

1. **No Woman No Cry** von Bob Marley and the Wailers bedeutet „Weine nicht".

2. **I Don't Like Mondays** von den Boomtown Rats. Hier geht es um den Amoklauf an einer Schule.

3. **Summer Of 69** von Bryan Adams ist kein Erlebnisbericht des 9-jährigen Bryan, sondern eine Anspielung auf die Sexstellung.

4. **The One I Love** von R.E.M. ist ein Gegenliebeslied.

5. **Hey Jude** von den Beatles hat Paul McCartney für Julian geschrieben, den Sohn von John Lennon.

6. **Born In The USA** von Bruce Springsteen ist kein Pro-USA-Song, sondern handelt von einem Vietnam-Veteranen.

7. **Every Breath You Take** von Police ist ein Stalker-Song.

8. **Roxanne** von Police richtet sich an eine Prostituierte.

9. **American Pie** von Don McLean – ein schräger, depressiver Text u. a. um den Tod von Buddy Holly.

10. **Freiheit** von Marius Müller-Westernhagen wurde zur Hymne der Wiedervereinigung, obwohl er beim Schreiben an die Französische Revolution dachte.

## Da weiß ich auch noch was:

1. _______________________________________

2. _______________________________________

3. _______________________________________

4. _______________________________________

5. _______________________________________

6. _______________________________________

7. _______________________________________

8. _______________________________________

9. _______________________________________

# Deutschsprachige Musiker, die es in den USA nach ganz oben geschafft haben

Wer hätte gedacht, dass diese Künstler es in den USA zur Nr. 1 der Billboard Charts gebracht haben?

Felix Jaehn
Milli Vanilli
Falco
Bert Kaempfert
Silver Convention

Ledernacken und Alphaville waren in den Dance Charts ganz oben.

Nena hat es immerhin auf Platz 2 geschafft.

Top Ten waren u. a. auch Kraftwerk, Scorpions, Enigma, Lou Bega, Rammstein, Harold Faltermeyer, Snap!, La Bouche, No Mercy und Cascada.

# Die fünfzehn besten deutschen Comedians

1. Loriot (Vico von Bülow)

2. Heinz Erhardt

3. Karl Valentin (und Liesl Karlstadt)

4. Otto

5. Hape Kerkeling

6. Anke Engelke

7. Carolin Kebekus

8. Dieter Nuhr

9. Michael Mittermeier

10. Johann König

11. Michael Herbig

12. Bastian Pastewka

13. Torsten Sträter

14. Max Giermann

15. Hennes Bender

# Es gibt so viele gute Comedians:

1. ____________________________________________

2. ____________________________________________

3. ____________________________________________

4. ____________________________________________

5. ____________________________________________

6. ____________________________________________

7. ____________________________________________

8. ____________________________________________

9. ____________________________________________

10. __________________________________________

11. __________________________________________

12. __________________________________________

13. __________________________________________

14. __________________________________________

15. __________________________________________

## Die schönsten Frauen der Welt

1.      Catherine Zeta-Jones

2.      Sophia Loren

3.      Selena Gomez

4.      Tatjana Patitz

5.      Audrey Hepburn

6.      Ornella Muti

7.      Sydney Rome

8.      Cameron Diaz

9.      Keira Knightley

10.     Salma Hayek

11.     Daryl Hannah

12.     Amber Heard

13.     Mila Kunis

14.     Christiane Paul

15.     Pocahontas

# Die schönsten Männer der Welt

1. _______________________________

2. _______________________________

3. _______________________________

4. _______________________________

5. _______________________________

6. _______________________________

7. _______________________________

8. _______________________________

Hier können einem zum Beispiel Terence Hill, Sean Connery, Richard Gere, Johnny Depp, Leonardo di Caprio, Brad Pitt, George Clooney, David Beckham, Ryan Gosling und Harry Styles einfallen. Aber diese Liste mögen bitte SIE ausfüllen!

**Modische Entgleisungen**

1. Hot Pants

2. Leggins

3. Midi-Rock

4. Schlaghosen

5. Plateauschuhe

6. Jogginghose

7. Schulterpolster

8. Neon-Schweißbänder

9. Flip Flops

10. „Arschgeweih"

## Mode, die keiner sehen will:

1. ______________________________________

2. ______________________________________

3. ______________________________________

4. ______________________________________

5. ______________________________________

6. ______________________________________

7. ______________________________________

8. ______________________________________

9. ______________________________________

10. ______________________________________

## Fahrgeschäfte, die wir geliebt haben

1.	Kettenkarussell

2.	Walzerfahrt/Rendezvous

3.	Halligalli

4.	Wilde Maus

5.	Krake/Polyp

6.	Raupe

7.	Affenschaukel

8.	Taumler

9.	Riesenrad

10.	Autoscooter

## Jahrmarkt/Kirmes/Dom/Rummel – an das alles erinnere ich mich gern:

1. _______________________________

2. _______________________________

3. _______________________________

4. _______________________________

5. _______________________________

6. _______________________________

7. _______________________________

8. _______________________________

9. _______________________________

10. _______________________________

**Wörter von früher**

1. Oheim und Base – Onkel und Tante

2. Eidam – Schwiegersohn

3. Trottoir – Bürgersteig

4. Blümerant – Schwindelig, übel

5. Brimborium – Aufwand

6. Famos – Phantastisch, hervorragend

7. Töricht – Dumm

8. Halbschuhe – Den Knöchel nicht bedeckende Schuhe

9. Nietenhose – Jeans

10. Schlüpfer – Slip, Unterhose

11. Heiermann – 5-DM-Stück

12. Radkappe – Radblende, Felgenabdeckung

13. Wählscheibe – die Nummernscheibe an alten Telefonen

14. Wonne – Genuss

15. Liederlich – schlampig

16.    Backfisch – Jugendliche/r

17.    Sich geziemen – sich gehören

18.    Hanebüchen – empörend, abwegig

19.    Am Sankt-Nimmerleins-Tag – nie

20.    Knorke – sehr gut

21.    Danke!

## Wörter, die ich kenne, aber kaum noch höre:

1.    _______________________________________

2.    _______________________________________

3.    _______________________________________

4.    _______________________________________

5.    _______________________________________

6.    _______________________________________

7.    _______________________________________

8.    _______________________________________

9.    _______________________________________

10.   _______________________________________

## Wörter, die immer falsch gebraucht werden/ deren eigentliche Bedeutung wenig bekannt ist

1. Busen – das sind keine Brüste, sondern der Raum dazwischen. Deshalb heißt die Bucht vor Wilhelmshaven ja auch Jadebusen.

2. Eine Olympiade ist etwas anderes als die Olympischen Spiele, nämlich genau der Zeitraum dazwischen, normalerweise etwa 4 Jahre.

3. Ein Luder ist (Jägersprache) ein totes Köder-Tier, das dem Anlocken anderer Tiere dient.

4. Public Viewing ist im Englischen die Aufbahrung eines Toten.

5. Covid-19 ist nicht das Virus, sondern die Krankheit.

6. Sich über etwas lustig machen oder sich selbst lächerlich machen, ist ein Unterschied.

7. Scheinbar ist etwas, dass nur einen Eindruck erweckt/Anscheinend drückt eine Vermutung aus.

8. Ein Guerillakrieg ist ein Pleonasmus (doppelt gemoppelt), Guerilla heißt schon „Kleiner Krieg".

9. Eine PIN-Nummer gibt es nicht, da die
„Nummer" bereits in PIN enthalten ist.

10. Mund-zu-Mund-Propaganda? Lustig. Es muss
natürlich Mundpropaganda oder Mund-zu-
Ohr-Propaganda heißen.


## Wörter, die meist falsch ausgesprochen werden

1. Accessoire, richtig: Akzessoar

2. Worcester Sauce, richtig: Wuster- oder Wurs-
tersoße

3. Afrikaans, richtig: Afrikas

4. Madeira, richtig: Madeira (mit ei)

5. Edinburgh, richtig: Edinborro

6. Espresso, falsch: Expresso

7. Rückgrat, falsch: Rückrat oder Rückrad

8. Bruschetta, richtig: Brusketta

9. Gnocchi, richtig: Njocki

10. Chorizo, richtig: Tschoriso

# Was immer wieder falsch geschrieben wird

1.    Herzlich Willkommen!, richtig: Herzlich willkommen!

2.    Sylvester, richtig: Silvester

3.    Imbusschlüssel, richtig: Inbusschlüssel

4.    Agressiv, richtig: Aggressiv

5.    Anullieren, richtig: Annullieren

6.    Rhytmus oder Rythmus, richtig: Rhythmus

7.    Stopschild, richtig: Stoppschild

8.    Ein bißchen, richtig: Ein bisschen

9.    Brilliant, richtig: Brillant

10.    Lybien, richtig: Libyen

11.    Labtop, richtig: Laptop

12.    Plazieren, richtig: Platzieren

13.    Krakehlen, richtig: Krakeelen

14.    Eifelturm, richtig: Eiffelturm

15.    Entgeld, richtig: Entgelt

# Fünfzehn ganz große Sportmomente

1. Max Schmeling wurde 1930 Boxweltmeister im Schwergewicht.

2. Erfolgreichster Athlet bei den Olympischen Spielen 1936 in Berlin wurde mit vier Goldmedaillen Jesse Owens.

3. 1954: Das Wunder von Bern. Der krasse Außenseiter Deutschland wurde Fußball-Weltmeister. Legendär auch die Live-Reportage von Herbert Zimmermann.

4. Armin Harry lief als erster Mensch der Welt die 100 Meter in 10 Sekunden.

5. Bob Beamon sprang bei Olympia 1968 8,90 Meter, bis heute Olympischer Rekord.

6. Ebenfalls 1968 in Mexiko überquerte Dick Fosbury die Hochsprunglatte zum ersten Mal rückwärts.

7. Ulrike Meyfarth wurde mit 16 Jahren 1972 in München Olympiasiegerin im Hochsprung.

8. Finale im DFB-Pokal 1973, Borussia Mönchengladbach - 1. FC Köln. Günther Netzer wechselte sich in der Verlängerung selbst ein und

hämmerte den Ball zum Siegtor in den Winkle. Sein Abschied vor dem Wechsel zu Real Madrid.

9.    WM-Finale 1974 im eigenen Land: Gerd Müller erzielte den Siegtreffer zum 2:1 gegen die Niederlande.

10.    Der gerade 17-jährige Boris Becker gewann das Grand-Slam-Turnier in Wimbledon gegen Kevin Curren.

11.    Es war im Viertelfinale der Fußball-WM 1986 beim Spiel zwischen England und Argentinien, als „die Hand Gottes" für ein eigentlich nicht reguläres Tor sorgte. Im selben Spiel folgte der legendäre 60-Meter-Lauf von Diego Maradona zum 2:0.

12.    Markus Wasmeier wurde 1994 in Lillehammer ganz überraschend Doppel-Olympiasieger in Super-G und Riesenslalom.

13.    Halbfinale Fußball-WM 2014 in Brasilien: Deutschland gewann 7:1 gegen den Gastgeber.

14.    Der größte Erfolg in der Geschichte des deutschen Eishockeys: Die Silbermedaille bei Olympia 2018 in Südkorea, sogar um nur 2 Minuten an Gold vorbei.

15.    Olympia 2022 in Peking: Das sensationelle
       Langlauf-Gold im Teamsprint der deutschen
       Frauen durch Katharina Hennig und Victoria
       Carl.

## Noch mehr große Sportmomente:

1. ______________________________________

2. ______________________________________

3. ______________________________________

4. ______________________________________

5. ______________________________________

6. ______________________________________

7. ______________________________________

8. ______________________________________

9. ______________________________________

10. ______________________________________

# Sportarten, die (fast) jeder ausüben kann

1. Wandern/Bergwandern

2. Fahrrad fahren

3. Schwimmen

4. Darts

5. Minigolf/Golf

6. Tischtennis

7. Schach

8. Stand-up-Paddling

9. Longboard fahren

10. Fußball-Golf

11. _______________________________________

12. _______________________________________

13. _______________________________________

14. _______________________________________

15. _______________________________________

# Technische Erfindungen/Leistungen der 60er-Jahre

1. Bemannter Weltraumflug (1961 Juri Gagarin)

2. Farbfernsehen (1962 Walter Bruch)

3. Kassettenrecorder (1963 Phillips)

4. Digitalkamera (1963 David Paul Gregg)

5. Taschenrechner (1967 Texas Instruments)

6. Spielkonsole (1968 Ralph Baer)

7. Computertomographie/CT (1968 Allan Cormack und Godfrey Hounsfield)

8. Laser (1969 Theodore Maiman)

9. Kunstherz (1969 Dominga Liotta)

10. Mondlandung (1969 Neil Armstrong und Buzz Aldrin)

# Fahrzeuge mit Charakter

1.     VW Käfer

2.     VW Bus „Bulli"

3.     Renault R4

4.     Citroen 2CV (Ente)

5.     Buckel-Volvo (z. B. PV444)

6.     NSU Prinz

7.     Opel Manta

8.     Ford Consul

9.     VW Golf

10.     Porsche 911

11.     Münch Mammut 2000

12.     Suzuki Hayabusa

13.     Simson Schwalbe

14.     „Tante Ju" (Ju 54)

15.     Trabant/"Trabbi"

16.     Jeep Renegade

# Ich hatte oder mag diese Fahrzeuge:

1. _______________________________

2. _______________________________

3. _______________________________

4. _______________________________

5. _______________________________

6. _______________________________

7. _______________________________

8. _______________________________

9. _______________________________

10. _______________________________

11. _______________________________

12. _______________________________

13. _______________________________

14. _______________________________

15. _______________________________

# Traumreiseziele

1. Costa Rica

2. Nepal (Trecking)

3. Los Roques (Archipel vor Venezuela)

4. Azoren

5. Pitcairn (am weitesten vom Festland entfernt)

6. Santorini/Thira (Griechenland)

7. Seychellen

8. Bora Bora

9. Cabo San Lucas (Mexiko)

10. Providencia (Kolumbien)

11. Amrum

12. Dubai (VAE)

13. Malediven

14. Carcassonne (Frankreich)

15. Grand Canyon (USA)

# Wohin ich noch reisen möchte:

1. _______________________________________

2. _______________________________________

3. _______________________________________

4. _______________________________________

5. _______________________________________

6. _______________________________________

7. _______________________________________

8. _______________________________________

9. _______________________________________

10. ______________________________________

11. ______________________________________

12. ______________________________________

13. ______________________________________

14. ______________________________________

15. ______________________________________

# Top-Sehenswürdigkeiten in Deutschland

1. Schloss Sanssouci in Potsdam mit allen Ne-
bengebäuden

2. Das Brandenburger Tor in Berlin – ein Stück
deutsche Geschichte

3. Schloss Neuschwanstein in Bayern – die ganze
Welt will es sehen.

4. Die Blumeninsel Mainau im Bodensee

5. Der Kölner Dom, Grabstätte der Heiligen Drei
Könige

6. Das Lübecker Holstentor und die Altstadt mit
ihren Gängen und Hinterhöfen

7. Das Ulmer Münster mit dem höchsten Kirch-
turm der Welt

8. Die „Wiesn" – das Oktoberfest auf der There-
sienwiese in München

9. Die Nordseeküste mit Sylt und dem National-
park Schleswig-Holsteinisches Wattenmeer

10. Das Miniaturwunderland in Hamburg, in der
historischen Speicherstadt

**In Deutschland gibt es noch sehr viel mehr zu sehen:**

1. _______________________________

2. _______________________________

3. _______________________________

4. _______________________________

5. _______________________________

6. _______________________________

7. _______________________________

8. _______________________________

9. _______________________________

10. _______________________________

11. _______________________________

12. _______________________________

13. _______________________________

14. _______________________________

15. _______________________________

# Beispiele für Lebensziele

1. Einen Baum pflanzen

2. Ein Haus bauen oder kaufen

3. Heiraten

4. Ein Kind haben

5. Goldene Auszeichnung (Sportabzeichen, Musikpreis etc.)

6. An Olympischen Spielen teilnehmen

7. Das Bundesverdienstkreuz erhalten

8. Einen Nobelpreis erhalten

9. Glücklich sein

10. Am Leben bleiben

11. _______________________________________

12. _______________________________________

13. _______________________________________

14. _______________________________________

15. _______________________________________

**Ich habe die Antworten darauf:**

1. _______________________________________________

2. _______________________________________________

3. _______________________________________________

4. _______________________________________________

5. _______________________________________________

6. _______________________________________________

7. _______________________________________________

8. _______________________________________________

9. _______________________________________________

10. _______________________________________________

## Berühmte Frauen der Geschichte

1. Kleopatra (ca. 69 - 30 v. Chr.), Königin des Ptolemäerreiches und weiblicher Pharao Ägyptens

2. Hildegard von Bingen (ca. 1098 – 1179), Äbtissin, Dichterin, Komponistin, naturheilkundige Universalgelehrte

3. Jeanne d'Arc/Jungfrau von Orléans (ca. 1412 – 1431), französische Nationalheldin und Märtyrin

4. Isabella von Kastilien (1452 - 1504), Königin von Kastilien, León und Aragón

5. Katharina II. („Die Große", 1729 - 1796), Kaiserin von Russland

6. Clara Schumann (1819 - 1896), Pianistin und Komponistin, Ehefrau von Robert Schumann

7. Marie Curie (1867 - 1934), erhielt 1903 den Nobelpreis für Physik und 1911 für Chemie.

8. Rosa Luxemburg (1871 – 1919), Vertreterin der europäischen Arbeiterbewegung, Gründerin der Kommunistischen Partei Deutschlands

9.	Mutter Teresa (1910 - 1997), indische Ordens-
schwester und Missionarin, erhielt 1979 den
Friedensnobelpreis, Heiligsprechung 2016.

10.	Malala Yousafzai (1997 -), Kinderrechtsaktivis-
tin aus Pakistan, Friedensnobelpreis 2014


## Berühmte Männer der Geschichte

1.	Buddha/Siddharte Gautama (563 - 483 v. Chr.),
Stifter des Buddhismus

2.	Konfuzius (ca. 551 - 479 v. Chr.), Philosoph
und Stifter des Konfuzianismus

3.	Aristoteles, griechischer Philosoph und Uni-
versalgelehrter (384 - 322 v. Chr.)

4.	Jesus von Nazareth, Jüdischer Wanderpredi-
ger, Stifter des Christentums

5.	Mohammed (ca. 570 - 632), Stifter des Islam
und arabischer Heerführer

6.	Christoph Kolumbus (ca. 1451 - 1506), Entde-
cker der Neuen Welt

7.	Isaac Newton (1643 - 1727), Physiker und Ma-
thematiker, entwickelte das Gravitationsgesetz

8.	Johann Wolfgang von Goethe (1749 - 1832), deutscher Dichter und Naturforscher.

9.	Charles Darwin (1809 - 82), britischer Naturforscher und Begründer der Evolutionstheorie

10.	Albert Einstein (1879 - 1955), Physiker und Entwickler der Relativitätstheorie


## Tragische Tode von Prominenten

1.	James Dean (1931 - 55), Schauspieler, starb nach nur drei großen Filmen in seinem Porsche "Little Bastard", auf dem Weg zu einem Rennen, als ihm die Vorfahrt genommen wurde.

2.	John F. Kennedy (1917 - 63), 35. Präsident der USA. In Dallas neben seiner Frau Jaqueline im offenen Wagen erschossen. Um die Tat und seinen vermeintlichen Mörder, der kurz darauf wiederum erschossen wurde, spinnt sich eine Geschichte um eine Verschwörung der Geheimdienste.

3.  Sharon Tate (1943 - 69), Schauspielerin,
    verheiratet mit Roman Polanski. Sie wurde
    hochschwanger von Charles Manson und
    seiner „Familie" mit 16 Messerstichen er-
    mordet.

4.  Alexandra (1942 - 69), deutsche Sängerin
    („Mein Freund, der Baum"). Sie starb bei
    einem Autounfall auf dem Weg nach Sylt.

5.  Elvis Presley (1935 - 77), Sänger, Musiker
    und Schauspieler. Er starb auf seinem
    Anwesen *Graceland* nach Medikamenten-
    bissbrauch.

6.  Natalie Wood (1938 - 81), Schauspielerin.
    Der Grund für Ihren Tod durch Ertrinken
    ist bis heute ungeklärt. Unter Verdacht ihr
    Ehemann, Schauspieler Robert Wagner,
    der bei dem Bootsausflug dabei war.

7.  John Lennon (1940 - 80), Musiker der Beat-
    les, verheiratet mit Yoko Ono. In New
    York von dem psychisch kranken „Beatles-
    Fan" Mark Chapman erschossen.

8.      Marvin Gaye (1939 - 84), Soul-Musiker.
        Sein Vater, ein Prediger, erschoss ihn mit
        einer Pistole, die er von seinem Sohn ge-
        schenkt bekommen hatte.

9.      Rock Hudson (1925 - 85), bekannt als
        Schauspieler u. a. an der Seite von Doris
        Day. Eines der ersten prominenten AIDS-
        Opfer.

10.     Andrés Escobar (1967 - 94), kolumbiani-
        scher Fußball-Nationalspieler. Nach seiner
        Rückkehr von der WM in den USA wurde
        er in Medellin erschossen. Spekuliert wur-
        de, dass sein Eigentor gegen die USA der
        Grund dafür gewesen sein könnte.

11.     Kurt Cobain (1967 - 94), Sänger und Gitar-
        rist der Band „Nirvana". Er starb in sei-
        nem Haus an einer Überdosis Heroin und
        einem Kopfschuss.

12.     Rudolph Mooshamer (1940 - 2005), Mode-
        designer, wurde in seinem Haus in Mün-
        chen mit einem Stromkabel erdrosselt. Das
        erinnerte an den Tod von Walter Sedlmayr
        (1926 - 90), der in München mit Messersti-

chen verletzt und dann mit einem Hammer erschlagen wurde.

13.    Michael Jackson (1958 - 2009), Sänger und Musiker, starb an der Vergiftung durch ein Narkosemittel, beurteilt als fahrlässige Tötung durch seinen Leibarzt.

14.    Whitney Houston (1963 - 2012), Sängerin und Schauspielerin. Tod durch Ertrinken in einer Hotel-Badewanne unter Einfluss von Kokain und einer Herzkrankheit. Drei Jahre später starb ihre Tochter Bobby unter ähnlichen Umständen.

15.    Zum „27 Club" zählt man neben Kurt Cobain u. a. Janis Joplin, Jimi Hendrix, Jim Morrison, Brian Jones und Amy Winehouse. Musiklegenden, die alle im Alter von 27 Jahren verstarben, meist im Zusammenhang mit Drogen.

## Beeindruckende Grabstätten

1. **Die Gebeine von Christoph Kolumbus** Ist er es oder ist es sein Sohn? In der Kathedrale von Sevilla oder im Faro Colón in Santo Domingo? Das geschichtliche Drumherum ist ebenso beeindruckend wie die Stadt in Andalusien und die Hauptstadt der Dominikanischen Republik.

2. **Kleopatras Mumie** Jedenfalls behaupten sie, dass sie es ist … Fest steht: Das Britisch Museum am Trafalgar Square in London (Eintritt frei) ist immer einen Besuch wert.

3. **Napoleon Bonaparte** Paris ist Paris. Und sein Wunsch wurde Napoleon schließlich erfüllt – im Invalidendom an den Ufern der Seine ist die Krypta mit dem Sarkophag zu finden.

4. **Jim Morrison** This is the End … Immer noch eine beliebte Pilgerstätte: der Pariser Ostfriedhof Père Lachaise, 6. Division, 2. Reihe, Grab 5. Bei der Gelegenheit kann man auch gleich bei Édith Piaf, Oscar Wilde und Frédéric Chopin vorbeischauen.

5. **James Dean** Drei Filme, ein „schnelles Ende" im Porsche und Weltruhm: James Dean liegt im Park Cemetery, Fairmount Indiana.

6.   **Heinrich Schliemann** Ein spannende Geschichte, die des reichen deutschen Kauf-
manns und Archäologen Schliemann. Beeindruckend auch das Mausoleum auf dem Ersten Athener Friedhof mitten im Zentrum der
griechischen Hauptstadt.

7.   **Taj Mahal** In Agra/Indien: UNESCO-
Weltkulturerbe, Geschichte einer großen Liebe, Gebetsstätte und Grabmal für eine Frau.

8.   **Tal der Könige/Pyramiden von Gizeh** Selbst
wenn man nicht auf Gräber steht, sind das Tal
der Könige bei Luxor (mit dem Grab von
Tutanchamun) und die Pyramiden bei Kairo
als letztes der antiken Weltwunder etwas, was
man gesehen haben muss.

9.   **Terrakotta-Armee** Mehr als 7.000 Krieger be-
wachen seit über 2000 Jahren das Grab eines
chinesischen Kaisers. Zufällig entdeckt von einem Bauern und als handliche Nachbildungen
auch bei uns für ein paar Euro zu haben.

10.   **Westminster Abbey in London/Petersdom im
Vatikan/Kölner Dom** Englands Könige, der
Apostel Petrus, die Heiligen Drei Könige …
wurden (angeblich) in Kirchen bestattet. Und
viele andere auch.

# Beeindruckende Künstler und Kunstwerke

1. Die Mona Lisa (La Giaconda) von Leonardo da Vinci (Anfang 16. Jahrhundert)

2. Guernica von Pablo Picasso (1937)

3. Der Denker von Auguste Rodin (1880 - 82)

4. Der Mann mit dem Goldhelm von Rembrandt van Rijn (um 1650)

5. Feldhase von Albrecht Dürer (1502)

6. Sonnenblumen in einer Vase (Serie) von Vincent van Gogh (1888)

7. Der Schrei von Edvard Munch (5 Kunstwerke, 1893 - 1910)

8. Venus von Milo (unbekannt, Ende 2. Jhdt. v. Chr.)

9. Girl with Balloon von Banksy (Pseudonym, geschreddertes Bild)

10. Pietà von Michelangelo (1498 - 99)

11. Seerosen von Claude Monet (verschiedene Bilder Anf. 20. Jhdt.)

12. Die zwei Fridas von Frida Kahlo (1939)

13. Campbell's Soup Cans von Andy Warhol (1962)

14. Verhüllter Reichstag durch Christo und Jeanne-Claude (1995)

15. Die Beständigkeit der Erinnerung („Fließende Uhren") von Salvador Dalí (1931)

## Kunstwerke, die mich beeindrucken:

1. _______________________________________

2. _______________________________________

3. _______________________________________

4. _______________________________________

5. _______________________________________

6. _______________________________________

7. _______________________________________

8. _______________________________________

9. _______________________________________

10. _______________________________________

**Ich ganz persönlich mag**

1.      Bücher aus Papier

2.      Schöne Erinnerungen

3.      Humor in jeder Lebenslage

4.      Berge von unten und von oben

5.      Sonne ohne Wolken

6.      Salzlakritz

7.      Urlaubsland Griechenland

8.      Gürteltiere (Armadillo, „Jere Jere")

9.      Aus der Narkose aufwachen

10.     Gute Quiz-Sendungen

11.     Gouvernanten-Look

12.     Sprachen

13.     Omas Sternchensuppe

14.     Echtes Teamwork

15.     Salsa (die Musik und den Tanz)

16.     Zivilcourage

## Ich ganz persönlich mag:

1. _______________________________________

2. _______________________________________

3. _______________________________________

4. _______________________________________

5. _______________________________________

6. _______________________________________

7. _______________________________________

8. _______________________________________

9. _______________________________________

10. ______________________________________

11. ______________________________________

12. ______________________________________

13. ______________________________________

14. ______________________________________

15. ______________________________________

16. ______________________________________

# Ich ganz persönlich mag nicht

1.  Stundenlang beim Arzt warten müssen

2.  Bunte Haare und weiße Über-Knie-Stiefel

3.  Einbrecher

4.  Hunde, die beißen oder laut kläffen

5.  Egoismus

6.  Kater (den am Morgen)

7.  Massentierhaltung

8.  Füße und Fingernägel

9.  Reality-TV

10.  Schneematsch

11.  Spinnen in jeder Form und Größe

12.  Wildschweine nachts im Gebüsch

13.  Gleichgültigkeit

14.  Umweltsünder

15.  Aufrüstung, Krieg, Gewalt

16.  Mathematik

# Ich ganz persönlich mag nicht:

1. ______________________________

2. ______________________________

3. ______________________________

4. ______________________________

5. ______________________________

6. ______________________________

7. ______________________________

8. ______________________________

9. ______________________________

10. ______________________________

11. ______________________________

12. ______________________________

13. ______________________________

14. ______________________________

15. ______________________________

16. ______________________________

## Was ich persönlich im TV nicht (mehr) sehen will

1. Impfspritzen in Oberarmen

2. Corona-Nasenschnelltests

3. Darmuntersuchungen

4. Köche, die aus einer Garnele den Darm raus-
ziehen.

5. Köche, die mit angeleckten Fingern in den
Kochtopf greifen – oder mehrmals mit einem
Löffel.

6. Füße und Nagelpilz-Werbung

7. Schlechte, ungepflegte Zähne, bei Menschen,
die sich Besseres leisten könnten, z. B. einem
Bundespräsidenten.

8. B-, C-, D- bis Z-Promis. Auch keine vermeint-
lichen Promis, die in Quiz-Sendungen de-
monstrieren, dass sie offensichtlich nie zur
Schule gegangen sind.

9. „Reichsbürger", „Querdenker" etc.

10. Kriegsberichterstattung

# Ich möchte auch vieles nicht mehr sehen:

1. _______________________________

2. _______________________________

3. _______________________________

4. _______________________________

5. _______________________________

6. _______________________________

7. _______________________________

8. _______________________________

9. _______________________________

10. _______________________________

11. _______________________________

12. _______________________________

13. _______________________________

14. _______________________________

15. _______________________________

**Zugabe: Letzte Liste. Was ich ganz persönlich in meinem Leben noch vorhabe**

1.    Costa Rica bereisen

2.    20 Kilo abnehmen, ohne zu hungern

3.    Ein Kochbuch schreiben (macht das mit dem Abnehmen schwierig …)

4.    Den 80. Geburtstag meiner Tochter erleben

5.    Fast jeden Tag glücklich sein

6.    Mein Glück mit anderen teilen

7.    1 x Karaoke singen

8.    Im Lotto gewinnen

9.    Nichts mehr von Corona hören

10.    Gesund und am Leben bleiben

Machen Sie sich doch auch eine Extra-Liste mit Ihren ganz persönlichen Wünschen, Plänen oder Lebenszielen! Es hilft dabei, sich trotz Alltagsstress auf das zu fokussieren, was einem wichtig ist – und macht Sie ein Stück glücklicher.

## Nachwort – Wir waren die wahren Helden

Wir hatten keine Mikrowelle, keinen Eierkocher und keine Kaffeemaschine. Keinen Computer. (Kein Internet, keine Mails, keinen Chat, keine Play Station, kein Facebook). Kein RTL oder Pro7. Keinen Airbus. Kein Last Minute. Kein Tetra Pak. Keinen MP4-Player im Auto, kein Bluetooth, keine USB-Sticks. Kein Smartphone (nicht mal SMS). Keinen Geschirrspüler. Keinen Mähroboter. Keine Sauna. Keinen Whirlpool. Kein Clerasil. Kein Mountain-eBike. Keine Inliner, Wakeboards, Curving- oder Mono-Ski. Kein DSDS oder GZSZ. Kein Ebay, Google, TikTok. Allerdings auch kein Aids und kein Corona.

Wir hatten Kalten Krieg, Sauren Regen, Contergan, Amalgam-Füllungen, die RAF, Pockennarben, Tripper (nicht persönlich), David Bowie, die Rolling Stones, Bravo und Dr. Sommer, Der 7. Sinn, Helmut Kohl, Hans Rosenthal, den Quelle-Versand, Waldsterben, den autofreien Sonntag, die Bundeswehr/Zivildienst (je nach dem), die DDR, „Darf ich bitten?" (und Damenwahl im Café Keese), Musikbox, Uschi Nerke, den Rockpalast, unterschiedliche Sandmännchen in Ost und West. Wir hatten Haschbeutel, Fransen-Wildlederschuhe, Vokuhila, enge Lederhosen, Günther Netzer und Ton, Steine, Scherben.

Früher war ich immer und überall der Jüngste und Dünnste. Heute bin ich ständig der Älteste. Und der mit dem dicken Bauch. Aber ich habe Erinnerungen. Das am häufigsten von mir gelesene Buch ist „Die Brautprinzessin". Der meistgesehene Film „Alexis Sorbas". Der Musiktitel, der mich am meisten beeindruckt hat, „Me and Bobby McGee" von Kris Kristoffersen, gesungen von Janis Joplin.

Diese Liste lässt sich fortsetzen oder von jedem anders schreiben. Entscheidend ist: Auch, wenn die Intensität der Gefühle im Laufe des Lebens deutlich nachlässt, kann man ein Tröpfchen Glückshormon auf vielerlei Weise abrufen. Es genügt, an die Fernsehserien von damals zu denken, um leuchtende Augen zu bekommen. Man muss es nur am Arbeitsplatz mal ausprobieren: Es genügt ein kurzes „Nano Nano!" (Mork vom Ork) oder ein angesungenes „Schönes Haar ist dir gegeben" (Gard-Song von Abba) und schon steigt dein Gegenüber mit ein.

Noch etwas: Als ich klein war, hatten wir einen Nordmende-Fernseher, so einen kleinen Schrank mit polierten Türen und glänzenden Messing-Griffen. Es gab das Erste, das Zweite und die Dritten Programme, alles in Schwarz-Weiß. Später kam dann (auch ohne den Knopfdruck von Willy Brandt) das Farbfernsehen, aber in meiner Erinnerung war alles, was aus der DDR zu sehen war, ebenso wie die Filme über den Krieg, die ständig in der Schule gezeigt wurden, immer noch in Schwarz-Weiß. Nicht, dass man wirklich darüber nachgedacht hat, aber unbewusst hat man wohl registriert: Früher gab es noch keine Farbe. Und in der DDR, in die wir Pakete an irgendwelche Familien geschickt haben, ebenfalls nicht. Das fiel mir erst dann auf, als ich selbst mit meinem R4 durch den Osten gefahren bin, nachdem ich versehentlich von der Transitstrecke heruntergeraten war. Eigentlich sah es nicht anders aus als im Westen …

Mitte der 60er-Jahre habe ich ein Bild vom Jahr 2000 gemalt. Mit futuristischen Häusern und fliegenden Autos. Auch auf den Wegen mussten die Menschen nicht mehr selbst gehen, sie fuhren auf Transportbändern. Ganz so weit sind wir heute, 25 Jahre später, noch nicht. Statt auf Fahrbändern sind wir auf Elektrorollern unterwegs und das erste Flugmotorrad ist jetzt auch zu haben. Obwohl die Entwicklung – besonders im Computer- und Mikrochipbereich so rasant ist, bleibt das Ergebnis noch hinter den Erwartungen zurück. Besonders, wenn man die Schattenseiten des Ganzen betrachtet.

Umso schöner, dass wir zurückblicken können in die Zeiten, in denen die Bilder laufen lernten und die Musik noch mit der Hand gemacht wurde. Wer weiß, wie man sich künftig an heute erinnern wird. Hoffentlich an, zumindest direkt bei uns, friedliche Zeiten. Denn bei allem technischen Fortschritt: Wer sich kaum weiterentwickelt hat, ist der Mensch selbst. Man kann nur hoffen, dass die menschengemachte Klimaveränderung der Evolution noch etwas Zeit lässt.

Mik Berger


PS: Noch Vorschläge für Listen? Gerne direkt an mich: MikBerger@gmx.de